LEARNING TO COUNT

ALBERTA T. TURNER

University of Pittsburgh Press

Learning
to
Count

Library of Congress Cataloging in Publication Data

Turner, Alberta T
  Learning to count.

  (Pitt poetry series)
  I. Title.
PS3570.U66L4   813'.5'4   73-13314
ISBN 0-8229-5249-1 (pbk.)

"Midden" first appeared in *The Midwest Quarterly,* Winter 1973, and is reprinted here with the permission of the editors. The Ashland Poetry Press kindly permitted us to reprint portions of "Learning to Count" from *The Strong Voice.* "Pod" was first printed in the *Southern Poetry Review* and is reprinted with the permission of the editors.

The publication of this book is supported by a grant from the National Endowment for the Arts in Washington, D.C., a Federal agency.

For David and Stuart,

without whom—

Contents

LEARNING TO COUNT

Backs walk away
bugs climb over
dogs nudge and trot on.

Children tumble in my sockets
and touch the walls lightly
but my hands are too large. I'm afraid
to lift.

Stones seem grateful
and vines don't break when I twine them,

but men don't walk here   and women don't
and God's too comfortable
to talk.

Bounce a quarter off the sheet.
                Stroke the fur   down   toward the tail.
Ease off the scab.
                If the dry grass wads too tight,
                jump back.
                There must be a nest.
O, unsigned rock!
                O blissful rooting in bins, infinite
                Mondays   pairs
                of feet.

Unwind string: cradle all cats.

Preparing for Siege

Peel a light,
core it, string it
and swing it from your hand.
On wharves watchmen will follow you, and across
fields, up cliffs to nests.

Outside dark windows, they'll wait
for you to fix that light, and when
you come out and walk into the barn—

At noon, hang it around your neck
and one or two will hang themselves.

So if it's yours, if you didn't lift it
from a hanging basket or a dog's mouth,
put it under your skirt.

A wall of helmets and cheeses and full casks
will be complete.

"Something wants out."
Should? Must? Just
does,
      rusts the lining,
      pouches over the belt.
You know you can rim it with your hand,
you plan: here the ear will be, there
the chin and the collar under the chin
(but it wants out, remember?)

You suppose it round and strain down
but the cage is bone.

So you go limp, you fall
asleep   on sand   and
ocean and sun and stone don't quite rim you.

So you dig or you drown

and you can.

Take

A honeydew with miniskirt and platform soles,
how long can you look without putting in eyes?
Or a truck with one outspread wing,
before chicks start scuttling under it?

Your house lowers its eyelids and yawns
out the side of its porch. Carrots
scribble your name, you erase
with a hunk of cheese.

In the spaceship Austin said to
Healy, "See that wrinkled brain?
Somewhere out here we must find
it a stem."

there's no one you have to speak to.
Put in a girl with short ears
a lazy brow.

Play a little deaf. That flat face
is opening its mouth, it's saying you've come
from a green lake (handing you a
blind white crab).

Home Free

The caves lack eyelids,
the trees are only trees with their arms up,
and all those lower lips are under rock.

Now sand settles feathers
over your basket.

The first place   for the first time
    (that log stapled to wire was not a fence,
    the tracks just blowing shut are not
    yours.)

You make no difference.

Threading

I

You wouldn't see the boy leading the horse
if the boy weren't naked
and you only notice the angel because
of the patch on its wing.

So I've bent my paper clip perfectly straight
and I'm threading it through your sweater.

II

He makes it seem easy
like stacking cans or shaking down pillows.
When he dumps his cart he always finds string
or a bit of wire for tying carrots.

Once I saw him shake out his socks:
two stones, one rabbit.

III

You've climbed all the steps
breathed through all the nostrils.
You dream the same train and jolt-jump
to the platform.

The coast was lava. You wore
that crisp vomit to slate.

But you're still crying, begging to be let down
on a long chain into the lava pit,
and you're cursing and sniffling because
you were hauled up
in time.

Midden

Find a midden containing bones, then assemble
  upper jaw
  right hip
  two feet:
a small female about to step.

Take the fresh carcass of a dog and place
its lower jaw just under hers;
cut off two paws
and put them next her toes;
break a bowl where her breast should be.
Heap up rocks, tamp down earth, scatter seed.

Later
  rain
  or a new dog
will sniff your midden:
"God-woman—
  dogs cut off two ritual paws for her,
  they licked her cheek,
  she squeezed her breast into the bowls they brought,
  they drank, they leaped,
        they danced off on two feet."

I

Why is every shop window dressed in white baby clothes
and where there's no water, all the roofs fly sheets?
Cars wait for old canes, and fish
fry with their heads on.

A trawler dips behind a wave
till only the mast tips show,
a sailor points, laughing, "There is no
danger."
A woman vomits all the way
from Tenerife.

Chew a cinder, taste garlic.

II

Lava ends in a brown kid
so new I heard its first bleat
(the mother curved her horns around it).

Lava—like rusty furnace grates
like cinders out of our old furnace.
Just touched it and I bled.

Lava breeds
lichen
then cactus,
terraces, a cow on each ledge,
then two cows ploughing
then widows with hooded heads
and a brown kid.

III

Caves, with doors and washlines
Sun
Crevices of black sand, slow surf with
paper cups
Sun
Dry dories in a ring
adobe church, plane tree
doors and windows shut against
sun

Six women dry on a wall,
six women shade a low wall.

IV

"We've lived in Kenya.   We tried Jamaica.
Came for peace.   No Blacks."
(bone scene   mackerel spine
camels ploughing   vines in pits)

Only to live   because someone started
(worm shells   nautilus
cinder sponge   salt bed)
"Christ's in the storeroom.   They're wiping the church."

> "Shot at Government House,
> and his dog beside him and his aide."

This was a lamb, this was a hen, this was a pig, this was a lamb, this

> "Stepped off the plane at Clark
> minus a leg."

and the price of beef and the price of veal and the price of beef and

> "For fourteen years she
> fed her husband horsemeat."

laid up for him a canter, laid up for him a gallop, laid up for him a

> "Someone else
> is buried in his grave."

so British, so beautiful, so British, so beautiful, so British, so

Your kite's riding the tip of an icicle;
you're teasing a gargoyle, braiding its snakes,
and one breaks off;
you shell your foot,
it turns black.

So you begin to notice mounds,
the skirts of islands,
the way pockets sag open at the top;
a sample parachute comes in the mail,
a ladder too long for its truck
flies a flag.

"In-
to Himself
descending,"
tiptoes down, the ladder rungs
cutting his pads;
damp tickles and makes him sneeze; he
feels for the last step, hangs
half-dreading oil, quick thought
of broken glass (he's thrown
some down).

Just as he lets go, you rake:

He's springing on cool stars down there
and smoothing him a curly pig; he's sliding up a long
bead; he's cutting him a clear
cube.

                under   over   through
turns
     humps
          breathes once
sniffles
     goes limp.

Won't burst, won't stand up
(has no edges to pry up)
is soft under your foot
is finally wet.

But was, oh definitely was.
    You keep rubbing the same spot.
    It's growing red.

Little eggs—blue, specked.
Laid, they grape;
feathered, they bead;
beaded, they
bird
    very small birds
blue or brown, bellied
in white.
       What they mean is small:
beak-bite, spur prick,
brittle
spike.

   *

I heard you,
MEAN!

Because hinge? Because tile's hollow—
and straws and legs?
Because feet have the soles of feet?

Pockets for tails. A tail graft in
Capetown has held three weeks.

   *

The soft part of conchs,
the stuff between shells.
I have bells of pods, necklaces of
teeth, but my tools
are spoons—somewhere a
pulp needs me—
a drying juice,
an unhoused snail.

    thumbs
    bells on your toes
    the lilac shoot scraping the roof

            (the Elyria water tank still reads "Class of 66"
            Jeff's old Christmas tree has just had cones)

    no sun all November
    light   out of the ground

Alaska: Three Ghost Towns

Valdez

Three Bendixes
on the hotel porch
and in the drugstore's ledger
mice between Miller and Muldoon.
Curtains behind "Danger, do not enter"
hardly need washing.

Iliamni

My print is three red grins in red
store sweaters, two white huskies
staked and snarling, and one woman,
her back broken
so long ago her neck curves up
like a healed pine.

My negative
is green grins on green shoulders
black wolves
and a healed pine.

Silver City

I take long steps
(ghosts need their naps),
I walk soft
(loose boards will curdle custard).

Outside, a sled with both its runners gone,
lengths of strap, roofless husky pens.
I reach in,   nothing
grabs my arm.

Knees

Fins, you're flicked shiny this morning;
picked off my screen, you leave fingers
and you're flipping again.

Shy glances, clean grins,
my knees polish from your praying.

How can I be good when you and the tips of bees
keep clicking and pointing and calling me
kind?

Pelt

Head-down on the barn door,
my fur dried flat,
my paw-pads firm black berries,

what other barn can mount so thick a brush?

Trunk

If you're lost, a bug is scrambling up your leg.

Wind moves your sleeve
because something sucks it;
You wait for cold,
but frost comes to curl the lips off chestnuts.

Perhaps fire, a chewing so
twig-by-leaf-by-stalk—
but rain, on its way down,
puts you out.

The bug   on your belt.

Muff

Today's one of the raining days,
not water,
but all the odd shapes:
up to your knees in roundish and squarish,

wet with rough, shiny with dull,
prickle down your arm,
not quite hooked;

one of the deaf days: "yes"   and "yes"   and
"what?"

Rug

Here's a faucet,
must I find its wall?
Must I owe the rattler for its tail?
I'd rather dream a tail and lend it one.
I'd say I had a tail,
I have a tail;
         or tell me tapioca,
fish need eyes, my father
is not drowned;

           the shapes I took for fences on the rug,
the pens for sheep, the collie at the rail;
the barn was locked, but he let me lift and lead grey Percherons in.
Milk cans went out, but I led Percherons in.

The farms I made were let stand for days.

Rim

Smoothing the long-haired rug,
setting acorns in cups,
pulling honeysuckle stamens to fat drops—

Lately the sun feels good on my back;
When I'm thirsty, rain swallows   and swallows.

The earth turns   just enough.

Wing

Time to make an angel
bowls   steam
        dough   heaves
                butter   leans
milk creams   oatmeal   breeds

hair—   sleeves—

Fin

Clear eyes on only a general map
don't see when the small town
in the crook of the right arm dries, because,
unnamed, nobody lives there, it has no
ponds.

Fins there   fin   as long as they can.

A FOX TOLD ME, "EVIL IS YOUR WORD:
THIS IS MY CHICKEN."

The pouch your children popped from
didn't snap back;
pegged from the navel,
the stretch marks hang yellow.

>   *Dolls grow more perfect every Christmas:*
>   *they wet, they speak, their heads come off,*
>   *and the strollers are collapsible,*
>   *and the suitcase packed for the cruise is open.*

Every time you leave
we find hairpins, thick black
ones, fine wire ones,
between floorboards, in the medicine
chest, once in the cellar,
in a jar of spikes.
In the nursing home they cut your hair
and tied it with a ribbon.
Something must be done—
One more hairpin, and we'll burn the house.

>   *Bone, Barbie doll, black rat,*
>   *get her a big chair*
>   *and she'll come sit with you.*
>   *One half an arm, the doll in her lap,*
>   *the bone in her side, the rat in her mouth.*

You want him born again?
He must learn to walk to "break his mother's back"?
Meaning the nipple was too small that first time?
Fish that hatch eggs in their mouths
must swallow   and swallow.

ask fools
bear stumps and the wings of stumps
come out of long tubes   come as girls and their briefcases
do not dim

earn horse chestnuts   call them buckeyes
    call them spiral horns   wax them
grind chalk   no   silk
    tongue it against your teeth   squeeze it
    between your teeth till the teeth squeak

haul the stick up   through   to your throat
join fur tips   join pine needles at their points
    stare back at sun

lean   see what pushes back   wood may be a breast
pack your nose with petals
pare onions   and again   onions
quiet blind birds   use stones

stem cherries   and the tree after cherries
    spring can't use old cherries

vow   where you can hear you
    where a man and a woman can hear that you hear
wait   for bark

X   cross

yes   you must

A Day in the Night Of

The moon too bright,
a planet larger than a planet,
and these things with three front whitelights
    and a red flasher going by with a
    high hum. One landed in the field
    north of us, but no one mentioned it.

On Friday, we left Wynn staring into space.
    Is he still there?

Yesterday the whole air force exploded
    over Rhode Island.

A large lung is about to inhale. It will
    be careful: telephone ants, tuck
    stray threads under the pillow, push
    dust motes from the air,

    hold back a thin strand of sun
    with its arm.

Hand

A Cherokee straddled my father's engine hood,
one foot in his hand;
he saw birch go by too fast
and nosed the old car through the stampede.

Father stopped driving when
they took the Indian
off Pontiacs.

"Came for fruit: heard
    of pods, strange cones, figs
    larger than figs,

Found maps, authentic burnt-at-the-edges ones,
    shelved, bottled, undecoded,

Was clued by one tipped bell tower,
clued by leaves tapered at one end, one
    end, mind you, and stones
    tapered at the *same* end.

Led: why else did meteors move from me
    toward this island? Why was grass,
    at night, always wet on this side?

And why else proclaimed? Why did wind
    push hair from your foreheads,
    land flatten, crumble, turn white, ribbon me
    to your tilted faces
    that inch forward?"

the garbage man is the Devil.
I believe every paper must be
            uncrumpled and the words
unwritten from the end and the can welded
            back over the corned beef; unboiling
the hoof will be hard and skimming the eyes
back into the wide ox face.

He will watch me do this.

"After the fire,
the child filled the crib with all his
toys—dogs, tin cups, half a bag of alphabet
blocks, a flat ball—so he could wake to something
his."

But it was my crib,
and every time I woke, something
                              had walked.

Sunrise, with Windows

They all stand at the window
because it will happen again:
after the candles, the wicks, the glass bowls of light
and all the quick shadows with sharp edges,
after the flames prick out and globes shrink
and they sit in their saucers like cellar fruit,
and the sides of the great bowl begin to shape—
the patches of white, the mud that peaks, the still
pockets that steam,

they crowd to the windows,
the babies in boxes, the snaggletooths
in elbows and feet, the cowls, the combs,
the plumed metal helmets—bumping, shoving
to look—

AFTER YOU DIED, I
RUBBED A SLICE OF BREAD ACROSS MY FACE,
AND YOU WERE THE BEST PART.

Learning to Count

"Count for: to be worth;
count in: to include;
count on: to depend;
count: to name, one by one."

I Crosshairs

Snake fence—peace sign—"Poodle Pups"
cords of bird baths and Virgins
hedge with two teeth missing

To the schoolbus, an armful of kittens

Meat
      (a dog's head?)
jet
pigeons
        wish I could like dying

> *"Patient has been extremely well during
> the past year, with no major problems
> except for the brittle diabetes."*

Waiting, I smoke the cars ahead;
exhaling guns them;
one VW can't climb it
unless I cough.

> *"Skin: in good condition.
> Nose: no congestion.
> Teeth: in repair."*

Angel tips on drifts
and trees turned stubble.

It was to have been
an egg with three yolks
or a python zucchini.

When milk freezes,
the bottle's supposed to leak.

> *"Extremities: no edema.*
> *Breasts: no abnormality.*
> *Blood sugar: elevated."*

Under the bridge a small car,
woman driving;
she's shifting gears, headed south.
At low tide I call down,
"Turn your lights on."
But tide's in, and she's
forgotten.

> *"EKG: normal.*
> *Chest X-ray: normal.*
> *Smallpox vaccination ordered*
> *(patient is going to Scotland*
> *for two weeks)."*

Man in my crosshairs!
Remember to aim left
of him.

II Female

The flowering tree she planted on the baby's
grave is no good.
Come spring, she'll hate it.

> *Thou shalt eat the tomato because*
> *the grasshopper has made a hole in it.*
> *Thou shalt press the sweaty collar back*
> *on the dried horse.*

He was born in November,
lived three months,
but he spends a lot of time with her in March:
"Not when I want him to, but
passing the rocking horse,
I know he needs to rock."

> *"Look for MARIGOLD SEEDS*
> *April 17 to April 22 on*
> *PEPPERIDGE FARM*
> *Cinnamon Raisin*
> *Bread. . . . Can be started*
> *indoors, but do best when*
> *not transplanted."*

"This one will be a girl:
  it will have brown hair and brown eyes,
  I shall not name it Carl.
  I hear its heartbeat everyday, on the machine."

> *The cat on your lap*
> *is the oldest living thing in the crib,*
> *the cat is female,*
> *this is the second swelling.*

III   He? You? Love Poem?

Frost and toast:

Telling you makes crystals start out on my coat
rain
run out of my mouth;
telling you is drawer slides and quart after quart
of milk.

If you deafen—moss over bone gongs—
and tray after tray of grenades
loads through wool,
how shall we count?

You tore out the wool.

If you killed me, I'd have no joy of it.
Yet I keep asking and
the soup skins over and
the towel smells of you.

Would you like to lie down?
Can I bring you milk?

I'm dreaming that squirrel again: the legs
come off; the chick I stepped on by
mistake oozed pink.

No, I won't bring you a urinal.

Kill the chick.

Needles keep me alive.
I hate my body
and your body.
Tell me snow is unclean.

Snow is clean.

He may have no face;
if he walks, it's on crutches;
there's phlegm in his throat.

But pain is not
what he's about.
He's a sort of foot, scraping
along stone.
Don't look,

don't talk about it.

Don't

IV Name

Knew it was swimming and swam for it, running
and ran for it—
    sifted
          dusted a city
dusted a cantaloupe
             dusted a cat asleep
                      a pigeon

  a beer can
        liked it

           On any old man
                    on any itchy baby
           or sick pigeon
           you could learn to count.
           The old man has socks; you can tell
           what color they were and what color they
           will be. He has jaws; they
           hinge open, they hinge shut. You know
           they will do that again. He has
           legs; every time he falls, he puts one
           before him and never the same one
           twice; he has claws—

I must love the woman on the bus who always
wants to feel my face
    and the fat driver who won't let her on
and the dog pissing my mailbox;
I must love the brown lumps on the back of my hand.

And when I find the baby rabbit dead in my fireplace,
I must scrape it out with the same hands

                              that fed it milk;

and I must   not   wash them.

> *You shall walk out in rows of tall corn*
> *your crotch will itch,*
> *crickets will scrape you,*
> *you will drink milk and drink milk and drink milk.*

> *All the stars must be named.*

In my dream I saw a foot,
longer than this room it was,
and the tops of the toes came to my knees.
It was white, blue white,
like the flesh of cucumbers, only finer,
like the flesh of radishes,
but finer than that,
and the veins that roped it
were dark blue and firm, thicker
than my arm and firm.

Where the foot rose and thickened
toward the ankle
a pulse breathed slowly
like a great milky lung, filling and emptying—

The toes were straight,
spaced wide apart and wrinkled like cheeks.
I touched one; it was warm
and dry and pushed back.

Pus   cheese   pin
     rain
milk

          milkring

     raisins
the hose jumps

         squeeze it
braid it   *not oil*
never oil

        stubble

   ox tongue

     sand
   NAME

And in my dream I squatted down and pressed my face
between the great toe
and the next one.

PITT POETRY SERIES